Poets' Corner
in Westminster Abbey

by James Wilkinson
Photographs by Malcolm Crowthers

Front cover: William Shakespeare, with busts of Elizabeth I and Henry V on the pedestal. Back Cover: Milton, Gray and Prior among other monuments.

Caedmon Chaucer Spenser …

How Poets' Corner began

POETS' CORNER IS PROBABLY THE MOST FAMOUS part of Westminster Abbey. More than 100 poets, dramatists and prose writers are buried or commemorated here. The name, Poets' Corner, can be traced back to 1733 when it was used in a book, *Poems on Several Occasions*:

Upon the Poets Corner in Westminster Abbey

Hail, sacred Reliques of the tuneful Train!
Here ever honour'd, ever lov'd remain.
No other Dust of the once Great or Wise,
As each beneath the hallow'd Pavement lies,
To this old Dome a juster Rev'rence brings …

Before that, Joseph Addison referred to 'The poetical quarter' in the *Spectator*, meaning the east wall where Geoffrey Chaucer and Edmund Spenser are buried. The west wall was sometimes known as the 'historical side' because the great historian, William Camden, was buried there in 1623.

The names of many of those memorialised here are known throughout the world; others, though famous in their day, are now largely unfamiliar. The size of their monument is no indication of their importance – with the exception of Shakespeare, who has one of the largest memorials, which none would decry.

There are no established criteria by which a candidate for inclusion is judged. To the question, 'Who decides who is to have a memorial in Poets' Corner?' – or indeed anywhere else in the Abbey – the answer is simple: the Dean of Westminster. It is one of the decisions which, by statute, is his alone. In previous centuries monarchs and wealthy sponsors were able to impose their will on successive Deans. Today the Dean consults his colleagues in the Chapter and, more widely, the literary world, before reaching a decision. Sometimes the decision is taken in response to a campaign by enthusiasts. Not all such campaigns are successful, however. A campaign to memorialise P G Wodehouse, for example, failed, even though it had the backing of some very distinguished people, including Her late Majesty, Queen Elizabeth, the Queen Mother. Occasionally it is the Dean himself who initiates the idea for a memorial. One of Dr Edward Carpenter's

Westminster Abbey – home of Poets' Corner.

3

Geoffrey Chaucer's tomb – he was the first poet buried in the Abbey.

ambitions, when he became Dean in 1974, was to see the First World War poets commemorated, an idea which came to fruition in 1985. Honour in his (or her) lifetime does not guarantee a poet a memorial here; of the 30 Poets Laureate who have been created since medieval times, only 11 are here.

It is rare for a recently deceased poet to be memorialised. Only four poets born in the 20th century have received a memorial: John Betjeman, W H Auden, Dylan Thomas and Ted Hughes. Only one poet, Robert Graves, was memorialised here while he was still alive: his name is included on the stone commemorating the First World War poets.

History has proved the wisdom of a delay between the death of a poet and the decision to memorialise him or her because, though fashion may favour certain poets, it is a fickle basis for judgement. Sometimes a poet's lifestyle or politics preclude him from being given a Poets' Corner honour – until a new generation has forgiven or forgotten.

The longest period between a poet's death and memorialisation is 1,300 years. **Caedmon**, who lived in the 7th century, is regarded as the first English language poet. He was a servant at the monastery at Whitby who turned sacred texts into poetry, so impressing the Abbess that she persuaded him to become a monk. He was finally given his memorial stone in 1966.

His nine-line poem is the oldest surviving poem in Old English and begins:

Nu scylum hergan hefaenricaes uard,
metudaes maecti end his modgidanc,
uerc uuldurfadur, sue he uundra gihuaes,
eci dryctin, or astelidae …

Translated, it reads:

Now let us praise the Guardian of the Kingdom of Heaven,
the might of the Creator and the thought of his mind,
the work of the glorious Father, how He, the eternal Lord,
established the beginning of every wonder …

The first poet to be buried in the Abbey was **Geoffrey Chaucer** in 1400. He arrived here not because he was a poet but because at one time he was in the royal household and he also lived close by. In 1389 he was appointed Clerk of the King's Works, responsible for construction and repair at places like Westminster, the Tower of London and various castles, manors, parks and hunting lodges. Two years later the Clerkship of the Works passed to someone else and he spent the rest of his life writing his 17,000-line *Canterbury Tales,* in which some 23 pilgrims to Canterbury each tell a tale to entertain the group. Chaucer was also interested in contemporary science and wrote a *Treatise on the Astrolabe* which he dedicated to his son, Lewis.

Chaucer had taken out a lease on a house in the garden of the Abbey's Lady Chapel in December 1399 but died less than a year later and was buried at the entrance to St Benedict's Chapel. In 1556 a little-known poet, Nicholas Brigham, acquired an early 16th-century grey marble tomb and canopy, possibly from a demolished city church, and installed it in the south transept. He had a picture of Chaucer and an inscription painted on the back (now mostly faded) and moved Chaucer's bones into it.

It was nearly 200 years before the next poet, **Edmund Spenser** (1553–1598), was interred here. Spenser was born in London to a relatively poor family, though he liked to hint that he was related to the Spensers of Althorp. The first edition of *The Faerie Queen,* dedicated to Queen Elizabeth I, was published in 1590; it combines Italian romance, classical epic and native English styles. In 1598 his house in Ireland was burnt in a rebellion and he was forced to flee for his life with his four children. He came to London, poor in health and spirit, and lodged at King Street in Westminster where he died in poverty.

HEARE LYES (EXPECTING THE SECOND COMMINGE OF OVR SAVIOVR CHRIST IESVS) THE BODY OF EDMOND SPENCER THE PRINCE OF POETS IN HIS TYME WHOSE DIVINE SPIRIT NEEDS NOE OTHER WITNESSE THEN THE WORKS WHICH HE LEFT BEHINDE HIM. HE WAS BORNE IN LONDON IN THE YEARE 1553 AND DIED IN THE YEARE 1598.

Memorial to Edmund Spenser – buried nearby.

He was buried near Chaucer, as he had wanted, in an impressive ceremony attended by many of his literary contemporaries including, quite possibly, Shakespeare. According to the historian, William Camden, they had written poems and elegies in Spenser's honour, which they cast into his grave, together with the pens used to write them. A memorial by the sculptor Nicholas Stone was erected in 1620 but this decayed and was replaced in 1778 by a copy. No stone marks the position of Spenser's grave and its exact whereabouts is unknown; a search was mounted in 1938 but the grave was not found.

With Spenser now lying close to Chaucer, the die was cast for this area to become a Valhalla for poets – and a place of pilgrimage for lovers of literature.

Shakespeare Camden Jonson Marlowe Hakluyt …

Shakespeare and other Elizabethans

THE MOST FAMOUS MONUMENT in Poets' Corner is that to **William Shakespeare** (1564–1616), though it was not erected until 124 years after his death. Shakespeare had elected to be buried in Holy Trinity Church, Stratford-upon-Avon, and at the time of his death there was no tradition at the Abbey of memorialising writers who were not actually buried there. There was a suggestion, later, that his body should be reburied in the Abbey but his epitaph, which he may well have written, makes it clear that his bones should not be disturbed:

Shakespeare's monument designed by William Kent and sculpted by Peter Scheemakers.

> Good friend, for Jesus' sake, forbear
> To dig the dust enclosed here!
> Blest be the man that spares these stones
> And curst be he that moves my bones.

Shakespeare probably disapproved of the way corpses were sometimes dug up and burned to make room for more burials. His monument in the Abbey was designed by William Kent and sculpted by Peter Scheemakers. It shows him pointing with his left hand to a version of Prospero's lines from *The Tempest*:

> The Cloud capt Tow'rs
> The Gorgeous Palaces
> The Solemn Temples,
> The Great Globe itself,
> Yea all which it Inherit,
> Shall Dissolve,
> And like the baseless Fabrick of a Vision
> Leave not a wreck behind.

Shakespeare is depicted as being relatively slim in contrast to his contemporary statue by the Dutch sculptor, Geerars Janssen, in the church where he is buried, which shows him as rather corpulent. (One commentator said the Stratford statue made Shakespeare look like 'a self-satisfied pork butcher'.)

Shakespeare was born in Stratford-upon-Avon, the third of eight children. His father was an important citizen of the town but later fell on hard times. William's interest in the stage may well have been stimulated by watching the travelling companies, The Queen's Players and Worcester's Men, who visited Stratford. He left the local grammar school at 15 and may either have taught or gone into his father's leather trade. He married Ann Hathaway when he was 18 (she was 26 and pregnant). They had a daughter and, later, twins, a boy and a girl. Altogether he wrote some 33 plays and much poetry – his sonnets, most dating from 1593–1596, were published in 1609. He helped to establish the Globe Theatre in 1599.

Over the centuries Shakespeare's memorial has gathered around itself leading Shakespearean actors. **David Garrick** (1716–1779) is buried here and on the west side of the south transept he takes a bow in a life-size memorial tableau. Garrick's memorial owes its existence to a young chorister at the Abbey, Albany Wallis, who drowned in the Thames, aged 13. Garrick was a friend of the boy's father and erected a memorial to Albany in the cloisters. When Garrick died the boy's father paid for Garrick's memorial in turn. Close by Garrick's grave lie the ashes of **Sir Henry Irving** (1838–1905) the great actor-manager. This was the first burial of cremated remains in the Abbey and followed a Dean and Chapter decision that there was simply no more room for bodies (the Unknown Warrior was an exception to the new rule).

In 1991 – more than two years after his death on 11 July 1989 – the ashes of **Laurence Olivier** (1907–1989) were laid to rest here. One of Olivier's last public performances of the famous speech from Shakespeare's *Henry V*, before the battle of Agincourt, was given from the Abbey pulpit at the memorial

Garrick's monument was sculpted by H Webber and erected in 1797.

7

service for Sir William Walton in 1983. It had the congregation enthralled. Olivier had rejected suggestions that the speech be recorded at the service because, he said, it was a young man's speech and he was now an old man. Sir John Gielgud unveiled Olivier's memorial stone in 1991. Gielgud himself had made it clear he did not want his ashes buried in Poets' Corner, but close by is a memorial to another great actor (or 'actress' as the inscription has it), **Dame Peggy Ashcroft**.

The historian and writer **William Camden** (1551–1623), who is buried close to the west wall of the south transept, had a special connection with the Abbey. He spent 22 years at Westminster School, one of the most prestigious schools in the country, first as Under Master, then as Head Master. He wrote an historical survey of Britain, *Britannia*, which aimed, in the words of the preface, 'to restore Britain to antiquity and antiquity to Britain'. Camden is primarily remembered for transforming the study of history, partly because he laid particular emphasis on the study of primary sources. He was made Librarian at the Abbey and, in 1600, wrote the Abbey's first guidebook, *Reges, reginae, nobiles* .... His love of music was reflected in his will, as he left bequests for the Abbey's singing men, bell-ringers and choristers.

One of Camden's pupils at Westminster School, **Ben Jonson** (1574–1637), is memorialised on the south wall. His father was a clergyman who died young and his mother then married a bricklayer; they lived in a narrow alleyway between the Strand and the Thames. Jonson was an arrogant man who did not suffer fools and frequently quarrelled with his fellow dramatists – though a kindly and generous friend. He lived apart from his wife, whom he once described as 'a shrew, yet honest'. One of his plays caused grave offence by its lewdness and he was imprisoned. He later killed a man in a duel and narrowly escaped the gallows. His plays included *Volpone*, *Every Man in his Humour*, and *Bartholomew Fair*. He was also writer of masques for the Stuart court, in alliance with Inigo Jones.

King Henry's speech from Shakespeare's
Henry V, **Act IV, Scene III**

This day is call'd the feast of Crispian.
He that outlives this day, and comes safe home,
Will stand a-tip-toe when this day is nam'd,
And rouse him at the name of Crispian.
He that shall live this day, and see old age,
Will yearly on the vigil feast his neighbours,
And say 'To-morrow is Saint Crispian':
Then will he strip his sleeve and show his scars,
And say 'These wounds I had on Crispian's day.'
Old men forget: yet all shall be forgot,
But he'll remember with advantages
What feats he did that day. Then shall our names,
Familiar in his mouth as household words,
Harry the King, Bedford and Exeter,
Warwick and Talbot, Salisbury and Gloucester,
Be in their flowing cups freshly remember'd.
This story shall the good man teach his son;
And Crispin Crispian shall ne'er go by,
From this day to the ending of the world,
But we in it shall be remembered;
We few, we happy few, we band of brothers;
For he today that sheds his blood with me
Shall be my brother; be he ne'er so vile
This day shall gentle his condition:
And gentlemen in England now a-bed
Shall think themselves accurs'd they were not here,
And hold their manhoods cheap whiles any speaks
That fought with us upon Saint Crispin's day.

As Jonson grew older he became bloated and drank too much. He lived in relative poverty in a house close by the Abbey and after his death was buried in the nave. It is said that when Dean Williams had assured him of burial in the Abbey he replied that he was too poor for a proper grave and that two-foot square would do for him – and that is what he got, as he was buried standing up. As his gravestone was being put in place a passer-by is said to have paid the stone-cutter 18 pence to carve the words 'O Rare Ben Johnson'. The same words appear on his memorial in Poets' Corner, put up in 1728 (both spell his name 'Johnson', instead of the more usual 'Jonson'). In 1849, when the grave of Sir Robert Wilson was being dug close by Jonson's in the nave, Jonson's leg bone was seen 'bolt upright in the sand', and his skull, with his red hair attached, came rolling down into the newly dug grave. Ten years later Jonson's skull was seen again when the grave of the surgeon, John Hunter, was being dug.

Marlowe's memorial window receives a polish before being dedicated in 2002.

Christopher Marlowe (1564–1593) was a latecomer to Poets' Corner. He was memorialised only in 2002, 409 years after his death, when his name was added to a stained glass window which had been installed in 1994 as a new way of honouring poets, because it was felt the walls and floor were already over-crowded.

Marlowe was born in the same year as Shakespeare, the second of nine children. Educated at King's School, Canterbury and Corpus Christi College, Cambridge, his first theatrical success was *Tamburlaine the Great*. Marlowe influenced Shakespeare and may even have collaborated with him on his *Henry VI* plays. Alfred Lord Tennyson called him the morning star which heralded Shakespeare's dazzling sun. Another description was less complimentary, calling him 'intemperate and of a cruel heart'. In 1593, at a tavern in Deptford,

9

south London, and aged just 29, he was stabbed above the right eye, possibly in a quarrel over the bill for supper, and died. The man who stabbed him claimed self-defence.

Marlowe's commemoration caused controversy because his dates, as given in the window, read '1564–?1593'. The question mark was inserted at the insistence of the Marlowe Society, some of whose members believe he faked his death at the tavern and escaped to the continent to continue writing, and from where he published his work under Shakespeare's name – a claim dismissed as nonsense by Shakespearian scholars.

Other writers of this period

Michael Drayton (1563–1631) was born in Warwickshire of humble stock. His *Ballad of Agincourt* contains the line, 'Fair stood the wind for France'. Though his epitaph describes him as a memorable poet, Oliver Goldsmith on seeing his monument said, 'Drayton! I never heard of him before'.

Robert Herrick (1591–1674), author of the famous line, 'Gather ye rosebuds while ye may', was commemorated here in 1994 when his name was added to the memorial window.

Richard Hakluyt (?1552–1616) was an antiquarian and geographer. His most important work was *The Principal Navigations,* which is a collection of accounts of voyages and discoveries by sea and land. He was educated at Westminster School and Christ Church, Oxford, ordained priest in 1580 and was a prebendary of Westminster from 1602–1616. He is buried in the transept, though no inscription survives.

Isaac Casaubon (1559–1614) was a classicist and historian. Born in Geneva, his Protestant family suffered persecution. He married twice, his second wife giving him 17 children, eight of whom died in infancy. The graffiti on his monument – the date 1658 and the initials I.W. – are said to have been carved by Izaak Walton, author of *The Compleat Angler.*

Buried near Chaucer and Spenser is the playwright **Francis Beaumont** (1584–1616), a friend of Jonson and Drayton, and his brother **Sir John Beaumont** (c1583–1627), though the position of their graves is unknown. Their names were inscribed on Abraham Cowley's gravestone in the 19th century. Francis Beaumont wrote a famous poem, *On the Tombs in Westminster Abbey* which begins:

Mortality, behold and fear!
What a change of flesh is here!
Think how many royal bones,
Sleep within this heap of stones.

Milton May Davenant Denham Cowley

Milton and the Civil War

THE CIVIL WAR BROKE out in August 1642. In religious terms it was a battle between Parliament which, among other things, wanted to do away with the Church of England hierarchy, and the Royalists under Charles I, who wanted to retain it. The Abbey suffered greatly, the choir was disbanded and in 1643 Cromwell's soldiers ran riot in the place, causing considerable damage and destroying the organs. It is hardly surprising, then, that after the Restoration of the Monarchy in 1660 there was little inclination to memorialise those poets who had been associated with Cromwell. The best known of them was **John Milton** (1608–1674). He had to wait more than 60 years before his genius was finally honoured with a memorial.

Milton was born in London. He was highly musical, could sing, play the organ and the bass viol. He was tutored

Bust of Milton from his monument by Michael Rysbrack.

in Latin, Greek, Hebrew, French and Italian, and started writing poetry at the age of 10. In 1625 he went to Christ's College, Cambridge, where he gave vent to his anti-Catholic feelings in a series of Latin poems. In 1641 he published, anonymously, the first of five pamphlets attacking the church prelates; he called for bishops to be executed and prophesied that they would spend eternity in hell. In a later essay he attacked the greed of the clergy. In 1642 he married 17-year-old Mary Powell, who left him after a few weeks and returned to her home in Oxfordshire. As a result Milton started to agitate to make divorce easier and when attempts were made to stifle his views he returned to the attack – this time deploring censorship. Eventually he and Mary patched things up, she moved back in with him and they had a daughter. In 1649, during Charles I's trial, Milton wrote passionately against the monarch and two weeks after the King's execution, Milton was made Latin (Foreign) Secretary.

In 1648 Milton had begun to go blind and by 1652 had lost his sight completely. The same year he also lost his wife and, six weeks later, his only son, John.

In 1656 Milton married Katherine Woodcock but she died shortly after giving birth to a daughter. In 1658 he began to dictate his religious epic, *Paradise Lost*. On the Restoration of the Monarchy in 1660 Milton had good reason to fear for his life and went into hiding. His arrest was ordered and his books were called in and burnt at the Old Bailey by the public executioner. At one stage he was imprisoned in the Tower but was later pardoned and released. In 1663, aged 54, he married a third time, Elizabeth Minshull, aged 24, who outlived him by 50 years. The 1665 outbreak of the plague caused the Miltons to move to Chalfont St Giles to the house where he lived until his death nine years later.

Paradise Lost, written in blank verse and regarded as one of the greatest works of the human imagination, focuses on the fall of Adam and Eve. When it was published in 1664, Sir John Denham entered the House of Commons carrying a page with the ink still wet, and proclaimed it 'part of the noblest poem that ever was wrote in any language or in any age'. In the 18th and 19th centuries it was translated into 18 languages including Russian, Czech, Icelandic and Tongan.

ABOVE:
*Detail from
Milton's
monument –
the serpent and
the apple from
Paradise Lost.*
OPPOSITE:
*Abraham
Cowley's
monument.*

By 1666 Milton had written *Paradise Regained*, which depicts the temptations of Jesus in the desert. Among his other works are *Samson Agonistes*, a play modelled on ancient Greek drama, and a *History of Britain*.

After Milton's death, Dean Thomas Sprat (Dean 1683-1713), who previously seemed to agree to memorials for poets regardless of their merit, rejected out of hand an Abbey memorial to Milton; his very name he considered a pollution on its walls. It was not until 1737 that a bust of Milton by Michael Rysbrack was at last erected in Poets' Corner, and a silver medal issued to mark the occasion.

While Milton had to wait for his memorial, another poet, sympathetic to the Cromwellian cause, **Thomas May** (1595–1650), was not only given a Poets' Corner memorial, he was also buried in the Abbey – but this was because he happened to die during the Commonwealth period. Initially, May had been a favourite of Charles I, but when his rival, the poet and playwright **Sir William Davenant** (1606–1668), beat him to the job of Poet Laureate, May became disillusioned and this led him to side with the Puritans. May came to an unfortunate end. After a hearty supper he tied his night cap too tightly beneath his chin before going to bed and it choked him in his sleep. His Abbey glory did not last long. His monument, and his bones, were thrown out after the Restoration. Then – the ultimate insult – his rival, Davenant, who had remained a faithful royalist, was buried in his empty grave. (In 1880 a tablet was

installed commemorating May and three Commonwealth preachers). Davenant used to claim that Shakespeare, who had stayed at his father's inn, was his real father. His productions were famous for their use of scenery and props on stage, 'raising it from the condition of a mere booth at a fair to that of an elegant saloon'. He was buried in a walnut coffin under a stone inscribed, 'O rare Sir William Davenant', echoing the inscription on Jonson's gravestone.

Other royalists like **Sir John Denham** (1615–1669) and **Abraham Cowley** (1618–1667) also had their loyalty and distinction rewarded in the Abbey.

Denham's literary reputation stems from his poem *Cooper's Hill*, which describes a beauty spot near Windsor. He had joined the young Prince Charles in exile abroad. On the Restoration he was made Surveyor of the Works and given a knighthood, but his remaining days were anything but tranquil. He was a drinker and a gambler; his second wife became mistress to his friend, the Duke of York. He had a mental breakdown, recovered and then, after his common law wife died suddenly, he was accused of poisoning her and found himself having to calm a rampaging mob who were after his blood. Denham is buried near his friend Cowley, whose tombstone bears his name.

Cowley, who was educated at Westminster School, was also a friend of Davenant. Like Denham, he left England to live with Prince Charles in exile after his father had been executed; on the Restoration he composed a song of triumph for the returning King Charles II. He retired to the country and eventually caught a cold from which he died. Though Charles II had not rewarded him in life, in death the poet received a magnificent funeral at the King's behest. 'Mr Cowley has not left a better man in England', said the King. Cowley rests near Chaucer, below Dryden's bust.

Other writers of this period

Sir Robert Stapylton, who died in 1669 and is buried here, was a Benedictine monk but later appeared at the English court where his Restoration plays were a hit.

Thomas Triplet (?1603–1670) is memorialised on the west wall of the transept. Born in Oxford, he went to St Paul's School and Christ Church, Oxford where he became a Greek scholar, wit and poet. He became a Prebendary in York (1641), Salisbury (1645) and Durham (1649) and was Sub-Dean of the Abbey. He established a school in Hayes, Middlesex, but it nearly had to close when he kicked a boy down the stairs in anger and the boy's father, a distinguished physician, withdrew his son. A primary school in Hayes still bears Triplet's name.

OPPOSITE:
The monument to John Dryden by Peter Scheemakers dominates the north-east corner of the transept.

Dryden Shadwell Butler Pope Johnson Gay ...

Dryden and the age of satire

ONE OF THE MOST PROMINENT memorials in Poets' Corner is that erected to **John Dryden** (1631–1700) at the north-east corner of the transept, just in front of St Benedict's Chapel, near where he is buried. Dryden was one of several poets whose work reflected the newly sophisticated culture of fashion accompanying the Restoration, and the critical scepticism which accompanied the intellectual revolution associated with Newton, John Locke and the Royal Society.

Dryden was a King's Scholar at Westminster and became Poet Laureate to both Charles II and James II. His huge output included his comedy, *Marriage à-la-Mode* (1673), his satire, *Absalom and Achitophel* (1681) and his famous *Ode to St Cecilia's Day* (1697). Much of his work had political undertones. Dryden's body lay in state, first at the College of Physicians and then in the Abbey's Jerusalem Chamber. Hundreds of people came to his funeral, which was chaotic. It is said that just as the

Bust of Samuel Butler who died penniless.

anthem was about to be sung, the son of Lord Jeffreys broke up the service on the pretext that it should be made even more splendid. Dryden's son was said to be so upset that he pursued Jeffreys until his death in the hope of getting his revenge. Dryden's grave remained unmarked for 20 years until the Duke of Buckingham raised a monument close by. This was replaced ten years later with one by Peter Scheemakers, paid for by the Duchess of Buckingham; an arch over the bust was removed in the 19th century. Dryden's great rival, **Thomas Shadwell** (1642–1692), who succeeded him as Poet Laureate, was buried at Chelsea and was the first poet not actually buried in the Abbey to have a memorial here. He and Dryden disagreed over Ben Jonson, to whom Shadwell was devoted while Dryden was only mildly enthusiastic. Shadwell died from addiction to opium which he had begun taking to relieve his gout.

Another poet from the age of satire was **Samuel Butler** (1612–1680), who was born of farming stock in Strensham, Worcestershire. The fifth of eight children, he was educated at the King's School, Worcester. Charles II was said to greatly admire one of Butler's best known works, *Hudibras*, which was a popular satire against the Puritans, though it did not entertain Samuel Pepys, who said he could not 'see where the wit lies'. It was said that the King never ate, drank, slept nor went to church without having *Hudibras* near him. If Butler was rewarded by the King, his reward did not last long, as Butler died penniless. With no money for an Abbey burial, he was buried instead in St Paul's Church, Covent Garden. His monument in Poets' Corner appeared some 40 years later, paid for by a printer, John Barber, who was Lord Mayor of London. A verse by Samuel Wesley drew attention to Butler's impoverished end:

'While Butler, needy wretch, was yet alive
No generous patron would a dinner give!
See him, when starv'd to death and turn'd to dust
Presented with a monumental bust!
The poet's fate is here in emblem shown,
He ask'd for bread and he received a stone!'

Butler was once described as 'an old paralytic claret drinker, a morose surly man, except elevated by claret when he becomes very brisk and incomparable company'.

Another great wit, some decades later, was **Alexander Pope** (1688–1744) who, according to his half-sister, 'had a maddish way with him'. He was born when his mother was 44 and is said to have caught tuberculosis of the bone from his wet nurse which inhibited his growth and affected one eye. Largely self-educated, fame came to him early. Among his best known works are *The Rape of the Lock* and *The Dunciad* – an epic on dullness. In 1715 he published the first volume of his translation of Homer's *Iliad* in heroic couplets, which was completed in 1720. His version of the *Odyssey* was completed in 1726 and an edition of Shakespeare was completed in 1725. He was buried, as he had requested, in Twickenham beside his mother. Though Pope wrote several epitaphs on Poets' Corner monuments, he himself was not memorialised here until 1994, when he was one of the first two poets to be commemorated in the stained glass window with the inscription, 'And Heav'n is won by violence of song'.

Pope was drawn to a group of writers, centred on Swift, who were close to the Tory administration. They called themselves the Scriblerus Club, dedicated to the ridicule of false learning. Voltaire said of him, 'I never saw so amiable an imagination, so gentle graces, so great variety, so much wit and so refined knowledge of the world as in this little performance.' In his life of Pope the lexicographer **Samuel Johnson** (1709–1784) says 'by no merriment, either of others or his own, was he ever seen excited to laughter'.

While Pope had to wait centuries before he was recognised in Poets' Corner, Johnson was told while he was still alive – though only just – that he was to be buried in the Abbey and was very pleased with the idea.

Johnson is one of the best known figures of the 18th century, his reputation particularly enhanced by his biographer James Boswell. Born at Lichfield, Johnson went to the local grammar school and then spent 14 months at Pembroke College, Oxford, but took no degree and fell into poverty. After trying his luck at

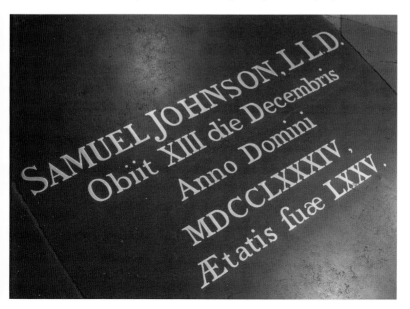

Grave of Samuel Johnson by Shakespeare's monument.

schoolmastering, he and his pupil, David Garrick, came to London in 1737. One of his first jobs was writing reports of Parliamentary debates for the *Gentleman's Magazine*. Johnson is best known for his *Dictionary of the English Language*, which he began in 1747 and completed in 1755. His idea was to provide a dictionary 'by which the pronunciation of our language may be fixed, and its attainment facilitated; by which its purity may be preserved, its use ascertained and its duration lengthened'. It contains many eccentric definitions. He defined 'cough', for example, as 'Convulsion of the lungs, vellicated by some sharp serosity'; 'oats', as 'A grain, which in England is generally given to horses, but in Scotland appears to support the people'; and a 'lexicographer', self-effacingly, as, 'A writer of dictionaries; a harmless drudge that busies himself in tracing the original, and detailing the signification of words'.

Johnson's other famous works include *The Lives of the English Poets*. Johnson met Boswell in 1763 and formed his Literary Club, which met regularly in the Turk's Head in Gerrard Street. He had a wide and influential circle of friends and was known for his wit, humour and a kind heart under a gruff exterior. Boswell's *Life* appeared in 1791. Johnson lies before Shakespeare's memorial. Johnson's own memorial was installed in 1939 and incorporates an 18th-century bust by the sculptor, Joseph Nollekens.

Matthew Prior (1664–1721), diplomat and poet, has an impressive monument designed by J Gibbs and sculpted by Michael Rysbrack. It incorporates a bust given by Louis XIV of France where Prior was for a time plenipotentiary. Described as one of the neatest of English epigrammatists, he was educated at Westminster School and St John's College, Cambridge. Among the sayings credited to him: 'It takes two to quarrel, but

only one to end it.' 'The ends must justify the means' and 'They never taste who always drink: They always talk, who never think.' Until the death of Queen Anne in 1714, Prior played a key role in negotiations with the French; he helped negotiate the Treaty of Utrecht. When Queen Anne died, the Whigs regained power and Prior was impeached and put in prison for two years, a period he used to good effect by writing more poetry.

John Gay (1685–1732) was another member of the Scriblerus Club. Born in Barnstaple, North Devon, both his parents died by the time he was 10 and he and his siblings were brought up by uncles. After leaving school he entered the drapery trade, where he made little progress. He began to write witty essays. In 1712 he became secretary and domestic steward to the Duchess of Monmouth, whose first husband was beheaded. His duties were not particularly taxing and

Life is a jeſt; and all things ſhow it.
I thought ſo once; but now I know it.

Of Manners gentle, of Affections mild;
In Wit a Man; Simplicity, a Child;
With native Humour tempring virtuous Rage,
Form'd to delight at once and laſh the Age
Above Temptation, in a low Eſtate,
And uncorrupted, ev'n among the Great;
A ſafe Companion, and an eaſy Friend,
Unblam'd thro' Life, lamented in thy End,
Theſe are thy Honours! not that here thy Buſt
Is mix'd with Heroes, or with Kings thy Duſt;
But that the Worthy and the Good ſhall ſay,
Striking their penſive boſoms——Here lies GAY.
A: Pope

Here lye the aſhes of Mr JOHN GAY.
The warmeſt Friend;
The gentleſt Companion,
The moſt benevolent Man:
Who maintained
Independency,
In low circumſtances of Fortune:
Integrity,
In the midſt of a corrupt Age;
And that equal Serenity of mind,
Which conſcious goodneſs alone can give,
Thro' the whole courſe of his Life.

Favourite of the Muſes,
He was led by them to every Elegant Art;
Refined in Taſte,
And fraught with Graces all his own;
In various Kinds of Poetry,
Superior to many,
Inferior to none.
His Works continue to inſpire
What his Example taught;
Contempt of Folly, however adorned;
Deteſtation of Vice, however dignified;
Reverence for Virtue, however diſgraced.

CHARLES and CATHERINE, Duke and Dutcheſs of Queensberry,
who loved this Excellent Perſon living, and regret him dead,
have cauſed this Monument to be Erected to his Memory.

19

he was able to continue his writing, but he felt humiliated because he had to wear the household livery.

Gay's *Beggar's Opera*, which opened at Lincoln's Inn Fields on 29 January 1728, was an immediate success and is still popular today. Many of its airs are taken from Purcell and Handel and just as with many of today's theatrical hits, it spawned commercial spin-offs including *Beggar's Opera* playing cards, fans and fire screens. Gay died after a short illness in 1732 and was buried in the Abbey with much pomp. Pope, who was one of the pall bearers, described him as 'In wit, a man; simplicity, a child.' He wrote the epitaph on Gay's monument, except for two enigmatic lines which are by Gay himself:

> Life is a jest, and all things show it;
> I thought so once: and now I know it.

Gay's monument, by Michael Rysbrack, was moved to the triforium in the 1930s after the discovery of an important medieval painting on the wall behind it. A similar fate befell the monument, also by Rysbrack, to **Nicholas Rowe** (1674–1718), who was Poet Laureate in 1715 and best known for his tragic dramas.

Other writers of this period

Joseph Addison

Joseph Addison (1672–1719), Oxford educated, took sides against the Stuart cause. He travelled widely in Europe and in 1708 became an MP. He wrote for the *Tatler*, started by his friend, Richard Steele, with whom he wrote much of the short-lived *Spectator*. According to Macaulay, Addison was a great satirist who knew how to ridicule without abuse. He is buried in the north aisle of Henry VII's Chapel. His statue (right) was erected in Poets' Corner nearly a century later.

James Thomson (1700–1748) was the author of the words of *Rule Britannia* which first appeared in the *Masque of Alfred* set to music by Thomas Arne. His monument, next to Shakespeare's, was designed by Robert Adam, whose body also lies in Poets' Corner – one of several practitioners of other arts who share space here with writers.

Gray Mason Goldsmith Burns Sheridan …

The seeds of Romanticism

THE 18TH-CENTURY POETS MEMORIALISED in Poets' Corner include Thomas Gray, Robert Burns and Oliver Goldsmith, whose collective work embodies changes in subject matter and language which span the transition from Classicism to Romanticism.

The memorial to **Thomas Gray** (1716–1771), on the south wall by Poets' Corner door, consists of a female figure (the lyric muse) holding a portrait of him and pointing to the bust of Milton above – or she would be if her finger had not been knocked off many years ago. Gray was regarded as the foremost English poet of his day as a result of his *Elegy in a Country Churchyard* which he finished in 1750:

> The curfew tolls the knell of parting day,
> The lowing herd wind slowly o'er the lea,
> The ploughman homeward plods his weary way
> And leaves the world to darkness and to me…

Gray was educated at Eton College and Peterhouse, Cambridge. After travelling abroad with his friend, Horace Walpole, he returned to Cambridge, moving to Pembroke College in 1756. The following year he was offered the Poet Laureateship, but refused it. In 1768 he became Professor of History and Modern Languages at Cambridge. Gray was buried at Stoke Poges, Buckinghamshire, the scene of his *Elegy*. **William Mason** (1725–1797) composed the epitaph on his memorial which links Milton and Gray:

Memorial to Thomas Gray by J Bacon.

21

'... he

fell

asleep

in a

ditch'

No more the Grecian Muse unrival'd reigns:
To Britain let the nations homage pay:
She felt a Homer's fire in Milton's strains,
A Pindar's rapture in the lyre of Gray.

The memorial to **Oliver Goldsmith** (1728–1774) is on the south wall of the transept, immediately above the entrance to St Faith's Chapel. Born in Ireland, the son of an Irish clergyman, he attended Trinity College, Dublin and graduated in 1749. Two years later he was rejected for ordination and instead studied medicine at Edinburgh and Leyden. He travelled widely and returned to London destitute, eking out a living partly as a doctor in Southwark. He applied for a medical post in India but failed to get it. He was one of the original members of Dr Johnson's Literary Club. Among his best known works are the play, *She Stoops to Conquer* (1773) and the poems, *The Traveller* (1764) and *The Deserted Village*. The *Vicar of Wakefield*

(1766) saved him from being arrested for debt when he sold the original manuscript for £60 – a sale arranged for him by Dr Johnson. Boswell, in his *Life of Johnson*, portrays Goldsmith as ridiculous, blundering, envious and vain, but kind-hearted and generous. He was buried in the Temple Church, off the Strand, and his monument in the Abbey, by Joseph Nollekens, was paid for by Dr Johnson's Club. Johnson wrote his Latin epitaph which says, in translation, that 'scarcely any style of writing was left untouched and none touched, unadorned'.

Scotland's national poet, **Robert Burns** (1759–1796), is remembered on the Shakespeare wall with a memorial unveiled in 1885, nearly 90 years after his death, and paid for out of shilling subscriptions by his devotees. He began life as a farmer, during which time he wrote some of his best poetry, including the well known *To a Mouse*. Among the most popular of his 200 songs are *Auld Lang Syne* and *A Red, Red Rose*. He was an extrovert, charming and convivial, especially with women. His love of alcohol may have accelerated his death as he fell asleep in a ditch after a drinking bout and

*The bust of
Robert Burns
next to
Shakespeare.*

developed a fever. Most probably the cause of death, though, was rheumatic heart disease complicated by bacterial endocarditis. He was buried in Dumfries. His birthday, 25 January, is celebrated around the world as 'Burns Night'.

Richard Brinsley Sheridan (1751–1816) is buried in Poets' Corner towards the centre of the transept, though he has no monument. He died in poverty but was given a magnificent funeral. When he was 21 he eloped to France with 18-year-old songstress, Elizabeth Linley. They were pursued by her father, who dragged her back not realising they were already married. Arriving back in Bath, Sheridan was forbidden to see her again. He fought a duel with one of her pursuers and nearly died. A successful playwright – *The Rivals* (1775), *The School for Scandal* (1777) and *The Critic* (1779) – he acquired David Garrick's share in the Drury Lane theatre in 1776. In 1780 he entered Parliament, managed the impeachment of Warren Hastings and became Treasurer of the Navy. Despite his distinguished life he ended his days in debt and misery.

Other writers of this period

Richard Cumberland (1732–1811) went to Westminster School and Trinity College, Cambridge. He is best known for some sentimental comedies including *The Brothers* (1769).

James Macpherson (1736–1796) lies close to his old enemy, Dr Johnson, who accused him of literary forgery when he published a translation of the supposed writings of the Gaelic poet, Ossia: 'I thought your book an imposture from the beginning.' Macpherson challenged him, whereupon Dr Johnson bought a thick oak stick with which he said he would repel violence. Horace Walpole called Macpherson a bully and Johnson a brute.

In the Abbey's east cloister is the grave of **Aphra Behn** (1640–1689). The author of 19 plays, plus poems and novels, she was the first major female playwright to write in English. Though not in Poets' Corner, she deserves a mention here as one of only eight women writers celebrated in the Abbey. The other seven are all in Poets' Corner (George Eliot, Elizabeth Barrett Browning, Jane Austen, the three Bronte sisters and Fanny Burney). Aphra Benn's epitaph reads, 'Here lies a proof that Wit can never be Defence enough against Mortality.' **Fanny Burney** (1752–1840) is the only 18th-century female writer in Poets' Corner and she was not so honoured until 2002, the 250th anniversary of her birth, when her name was included in the memorial window. Among her writings is her personal account of undergoing a mastectomy without anaesthetic. Burney has a family connection in the Abbey as her father, Charles Burney (1726–1814), the musicologist, is memorialised in the north choir aisle. Fanny was a friend of Dr Johnson and author of the best-seller *Evelina* (1778), a book recently described as the *Bridget Jones's Diary* of the age. Burney was to influence many women writers including Jane Austen. She is buried at Walcot, Bath.

~Poets' Corner~

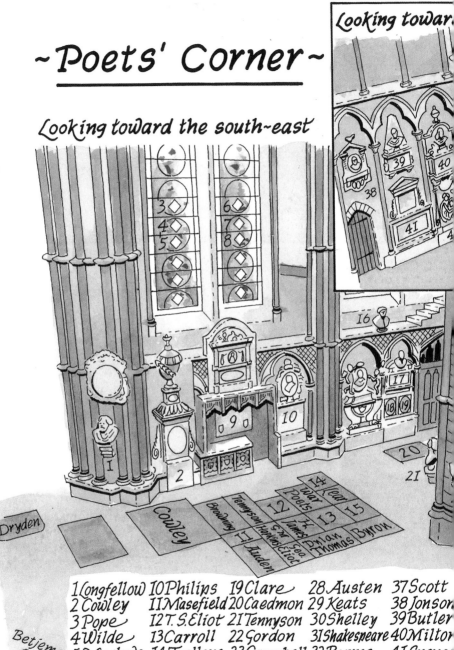

Looking toward the south~east

Looking towar...

Dryden

Cowley

Betjeman

Blake

1 Longfellow | 10 Philips | 19 Clare | 28 Austen | 37 Scott
2 Cowley | 11 Masefield | 20 Caedmon | 29 Keats | 38 Jonson
3 Pope | 12 T. S. Eliot | 21 Tennyson | 30 Shelley | 39 Butler
4 Wilde | 13 Carroll | 22 Gordon | 31 Shakespeare | 40 Milton
5 Marlowe | 14 Trollope | 23 Campbell | 32 Burns | 41 Spence
6 Herrick | 15 Lawrence | 24 Wordsworth | 33 Thomson | 42 Gray
7 Housman | 16 Arnold | 25 Coleridge | 34 Brontes | 43 Shadw
8 Burney | 17 Drayton | 26 Southey | 35 Goldsmith | 44 Mason
9 Chaucer | 18 Arnold | 27 Johnson | 36 Ruskin | 45 Prior

south~west

45 46 47 21 23

36 37 48 49 50 51 52 53

29 30 32 26 33 27 34 28 31 24

35 36 37

Olivier
Irving Ashcroft

Garrick
Johnson
Sheridan
Cumberland
Dickens
Hardy Kipling
Handel

St. Denis
Sharp
Handel
Thackeray
Addison
Macaulay
Barrow
Keble

Macaulay

A 0407

Blake Wordsworth Coleridge Southey Shelley ...

The Romantic Movement

THE ORIGINS OF ROMANTICISM are perceptible in the last quarter of the 18th century; it reached its height in the first quarter of the 19th. A reaction against the earlier formal Classicism, it represented a European-wide shift of sensibility involving language, nature, politics and society.

William Blake (1757–1827) is a relative latecomer to Poets' Corner and the most recent to have a likeness in the form of a bust installed in the Abbey. It is by Sir Jacob Epstein and was placed here in 1957 on the 200th anniversary of his birth. Blake was the son of a London hosier. Instead of going to school he was apprenticed to an engraver – a training which enabled him to engrave his poems and illustrate them. In his thirties his poetry began to reveal his extraordinarily mystical state of mind. He sketched for hours in the Abbey where, he would claim, he could see ghostly processions of pilgrims: he was surprised no-one else could see them. He wrote of divine love, the power of evil and the need to challenge authority. His best known poem is probably *Jerusalem*, which is sung famously as a hymn. His *Songs of Experience* contains his poem which begins:

THIS PAGE:
Jacob Epstein's bust of William Blake.

OPPOSITE:
William Wordsworth in pensive mood.

Tyger! Tyger! burning bright
In the forests of the night,
What immortal hand or eye
Could frame thy fearful symmetry?

In August 1817 the *Edinburgh Review* referred to a group of three poets who lived in the Lake District as the 'Lake Poets'. It was a term which stuck. The poets were Wordsworth, Coleridge and Southey, all three of whom are memorialised in Poets' Corner.

William Wordsworth (1770–1850), though now revered, was not always so well-liked. Some of his poetry was received with great hostility by critics at the time. Born in Cockermouth in Cumbria, he was locally educated and then went to St John's College, Cambridge. In 1790 he travelled in France and Italy and became enthusiastic about Republicanism, as his travels coincided with the French Revolution, though this enthusiasm was not to last. In 1795 he formed a friendship with Samuel Taylor Coleridge and worked closely with him, jointly publishing, in 1798, *Lyrical Ballads,* which marked a revival in English poetry. In 1799 he settled, with his sister, Dorothy, at Grasmere in the Lake District, where he spent the rest of his life. For many years he had a job as distributor of stamps for Westmoreland, which gave him an income and eventually a pension. In 1843 he succeeded Robert Southey as Poet Laureate. His most popular works are his poem *Daffodils* and his poem composed *On Westminster Bridge* which starts 'Earth has not anything to show more fair'. His statue, by Frederick Thrupp, was originally in the south-west tower chapel but in 1932 was moved to its present position in Poets' Corner.

Samuel Taylor Coleridge (1772–1834) was the son of the Vicar of Ottery St Mary in Devon. Educated at Christ's Hospital and Jesus College, Cambridge, he went to London, enlisted, was discharged shortly afterwards and returned to Cambridge. He became friendly with Robert Southey and they married two sisters. In 1795 he met Wordsworth and they became firm friends – their *Lyrical Ballads* contained Coleridge's best known work, *The Rime of the Ancient Mariner.* Another of his famous poems, *Kubla Khan,* he wrote in 1797 while under the influence of opium, to which he eventually became addicted and which led to a downward spiral: in 1808 he even abandoned his family. He

Jane Austen's memorial is tiny compared with the one in Winchester Cathedral where she is buried.

is buried in Highgate Cemetery. The bust in Poets' Corner was unveiled in 1885 by James Russell Lowell, a United States Minister, on behalf of the American benefactor who paid for it, a Dr Mercer.

Robert Southey (1774–1843) was expelled from Westminster School after writing an attack on corporal punishment. Educated at Balliol College, Oxford, he became friendly with Coleridge and settled in Keswick in the Lake District. In 1813 he became Poet Laureate. He wrote a prodigious amount but today is best remembered for some of his shorter poems, including *The Battle of Blenheim* and *The Inchcape Rock*. He also wrote biographies of Nelson (1813), Wesley (1820), the poet Cowper (1833-7) and a history of Brazil. His bust is high up on the Shakespeare wall.

Other poets of the Romantic Movement commemorated here include Shelley, Keats and Byron.

Percy Bysshe Shelley (1792–1822) was described as 'a dazzling revolutionary comet' of the Romantic Movement. Born to wealthy respectable parents (his father was an MP) he was educated at Eton and University College, Oxford. But he was a rebel and was sent down for circulating a pamphlet on *The Necessity of Atheism*; he also advocated republicanism and free love. His first wife, Harriet, whom he married when she was 16, drowned herself in the Serpentine and he married again, Mary Godwin, the author of *Frankenstein*. He travelled widely and in 1816 became friendly with Byron: together they formed a literary colony in Pisa. His best known work, the lyrical drama *Prometheus Unbound*, was published in 1820. His greatest odes and lyrics were written in his last few years and include *To a Skylark*, *To the West Wind* and *The Cloud*. Shelley drowned in the bay of Spezia while sailing, aged just 30. His body was burned on the beach, an event witnessed by Byron who wrote to a friend, 'You can have no idea what an extraordinary effect a funeral pyre has on a desolate shore, with mountains in the background and the sea before, and the singular appearance the salt and frankincense gave to the flame. All of Shelley was consumed, except his heart which would not take the flame and is now preserved in spirits of wine.' His ashes were buried in the Protestant cemetery in Rome; his heart was buried in St Peter's Church, Bournemouth, Dorset. At the time he was refused a memorial in Poets' Corner because of his atheism.

Meanwhile, his almost exact contemporary, **John Keats** (1795–1821), had trained as an apothecary and then a surgeon before opting to write poetry and becoming one of the great Romantics. In 1817 Shelley helped him publish *Poems by John Keats*. It was not a success but the following year he wrote *Endymion*, which he described as 'a feverish attempt rather than a deed accomplished'. His great odes include, *To a Grecian Urn* and *To a Nightingale*. He died in Rome of consumption. The Keats–Shelley Association paid for memorials to both men and in 1945 the two tablets on the Shakespeare wall, linked with a marble swag, were unveiled by John Masefield.

For many years the third member of the group, **Lord (George Gordon) Byron** (1788–1824), was excluded from Poets' Corner because of his scandalous life-style. He came into his title when he was 10. Educated at Harrow, where he was described as a rough, curly-headed boy, and Trinity College, Cambridge, he is best known for his work, *Childe Harold's Pilgrimage*. In 1815 he married an heiress from whom he separated the following year. He left England, complaining about its hypocrisy, and never returned, spending much of his time in Venice, Ravenna, Pisa and Genoa. He became a romantic hero to many. In 1823 he set out to join the Greek insurgents in their fight against Turkey and died of fever the following year in Missolonghi. Some wanted him buried in the Abbey but Dean John Ireland refused and he is buried at Hucknall Torkard in Nottinghamshire. In 1924, on the centenary of his death, a petition from many distinguished men of letters for an Abbey memorial was turned down by Dean Herbert Ryle, who said that Byron 'partly by his openly dissolute life and partly by the influence of his licentious verse, earned a world-wide reputation for immorality among English-speaking people'. Eventually, in 1969, a white marble floor stone was unveiled to his memory.

Robert Southey's bust – close to Shakespeare.

Jane Austen (1775–1817) is one of the seven women writers honoured in Poets' Corner and has a small plaque which was unveiled in 1967. The daughter of a country clergyman, she lived in Bath, Southampton, Chawton in Hampshire and finally close to Winchester Cathedral, where she is buried. Her writing reflected the social lifestyle of a small household at the time. Her output was not great but all her books are much-loved classics: *Sense and Sensibility* (1811), *Pride and Prejudice* (1813), *Mansfield Park* (1814), *Emma* (1816), *Northanger Abbey* (1818) and *Persuasion* (1818), though she did not write them in that order.

John Keble (1792–1866), memorialised on the west wall, was educated at Corpus Christi College, Oxford. He followed his father into the priesthood and was made a Fellow of Oriel College, Oxford in 1811; in 1827 he published *The Christian Year* which became very popular. He was elected Professor of Poetry at Oxford in 1831 and with his colleagues, Pusey and Newman, he was one of the founders of the Oxford Movement. Keble College, Oxford, was named in his honour.

The memorial to **John Clare** (1793–1864) is on the east wall by Poets' Corner door and was unveiled in 1989. He began life as a farm labourer and in 1820 he published one of his best known works, *Poems Descriptive of Rural Life*. He spent the last 27 years of his life in a lunatic asylum but continued to pour out his poetry. He is buried at Helpston, Northamptonshire.

Thomas Babington Macaulay (Lord Macaulay) (1800–1859) is buried at the foot of Addison's statue and his bust is close by. The precocious son of the anti-slavery campaigner, Zachary Macaulay (commemorated in the north-west tower chapel). Young Thomas liked reading the Bible. As a little child he once took exception to a maid who threw away some oyster shells with which he had marked out a plot in the garden. He came into his mother's drawing room saying, 'Cursed be Sally, for it is written, cursed is he that removeth his neighbour's landmarks.' Thomas became a politician and brilliant historian, his *History of England* being very popular.

Henry Wadsworth Longfellow (1807–1882) was the first American to be honoured in Poets' Corner. Born in Maine, he went to Harvard, where he eventually became Professor of Modern Languages. His second wife was burnt to death in an accident involving lighted sealing wax. He visited London in 1842 and was the guest of Dickens. On his return voyage he wrote his *Poems on Slavery* which reflected his disgust at the slave trade. His best known work is *Hiawatha*. His bust was placed in Poets' Corner in 1884 by his British admirers.

Alfred Lord Tennyson (1809–1892) was the last poet whose body was buried in the Abbey (since then only ashes have been placed here). A clergyman's son, he went to Trinity College, Cambridge. In 1850 he succeeded Wordsworth as Poet Laureate. Among his best known works are *In Memoriam*, in which he mourns a lost friend, *Morte d'Arthur* and *The Charge of the Light Brigade*. As Tennyson lay dying, his hand rested on his Shakespeare opened at *Cymbeline*, which he tried to read but failed; the book was placed with him in his coffin. His bust, by Thomas Woolner, was set up in 1895.

Sir Walter Scott (1771–1832) was born in Edinburgh. His works include *The Lady of the Lake* and *The Lord of the Isles*, and his many novels, initially published anonymously, include *Waverley* and *Ivanhoe*. In 1813 he refused the offer of the Poet Laureateship in favour of Robert Southey.

Dickens Lear Trollope Carroll Brontes Eliot …

More Victorians

THE GRAVE OF **Charles Dickens** (1812–1870) is one of the most sought after by visitors to the Abbey. He was to be buried in Rochester Cathedral but shortly before the funeral the public wish that he be buried in Westminster Abbey prevailed, his executors agreeing on condition that the funeral was private. Only about a dozen attended, nine of whom were Abbey personnel, but afterwards the Dean threw open the doors of the Abbey so that people could come and pay their respects at the open grave. The queues were long. When the doors finally closed, many of the bunches of flowers people had placed in the grave were found to be wrapped in scraps of cloth – tributes from the poor who had come to honour their hero.

Dickens' father was a Government clerk who was at one time incarcerated in the Marshalsea prison for debt. This had a profound effect on his son, who reflected some of these experiences in *David Copperfield* (1849–50). He had little education. One of his early jobs was reporting on the debates in the House of Commons for the *Morning Chronicle*. His first book, published as a periodical

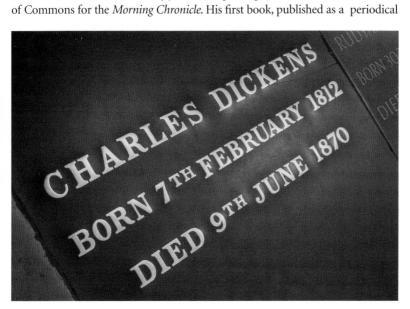

LEFT:
*Grave of
Charles
Dickens.*
OPPOSITE:
*Busts of
Longfellow,
Tennyson
and Scott.*

31

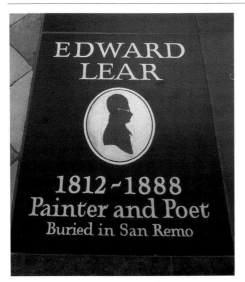

EDWARD LEAR

1812-1888
Painter and Poet
Buried in San Remo

Edward Lear's memorial stone was unveiled in 1988 on the centenary of his death.

in 20 monthly instalments, was *The Pickwick Papers*, which he wrote when he was 24. Others soon followed, including *Oliver Twist* (1837–8), *Nicholas Nickleby* (1838–9) and *Dombey and Son* (1849–50). Dickens was also a performer and in 1858 he began to give public readings of his works. He died before finishing his last book, *Edwin Drood*. Dickens requested no memorial: instead it was his wish that 'My name be inscribed in plain English letters on my tomb. I rest my claim to the remembrance of my country upon my published works'. Not everyone was delighted to see Dickens in Poet's Corner. The Victorian writer and artist, Samuel Butler, commented disparagingly, 'They have buried Dickens cheek-by-jowl in the very next grave to Handel. I should not mind, I suppose, but it saddens me that people who can do such things can become Deans of Westminster.'

The floor stone memorial to **Edward Lear** (1812–1888) shows his profile and was unveiled by Sir Hugh Casson in 1988. Lear was born in the same year as Dickens but his work could not have been more different. He was the 20th child of a London stockbroker and highly talented both as writer and artist – he even taught drawing to the Royal Family. He did much to popularise the limerick: his *Book of Nonsense* (1846) was written to amuse the grandchildren of his patron, the Earl of Derby. He also wrote *Nonsense Songs, Stories and Botany* (1870). His best known nonsense poem is *The Owl and the Pussycat*. His health was poor – he was epileptic and suffered from depression – and partly for the sake of his health he lived in Italy, where he is buried.

Close by Edward Lear's memorial is one to **Anthony Trollope** (1815–1882) which was unveiled by Prime Minister John Major in 1993. On it is inscribed the last line of his autobiography: 'Now I stretch out my hand and from the further shore I bid adieu to all who have cared to read any among the many words that I have written.'

Trollope was educated at Harrow and Winchester, but when his father's debts became unsustainable the family moved to Belgium. He worked for the General Post Office from 1834, where one of his innovations was the invention of the pillar box. His Barsetshire stories, of which the first was *The Warden* (1855), were to become his most popular works.

Lewis Carroll (1832–1898), whose real name was Charles Lutwidge Dodgson, was another author, like Lear, with a special appeal to children. His most famous book, *Alice's Adventures in Wonderland* (1865), began as a story told on a river trip to Alice Liddell, the daughter of his friend, Henry Liddell, Dean of Christ

Church at the time, who had been Head Master of Westminster School, where Alice was born, from 1846–55. It was followed by *Through the Looking Glass* (1872). His memorial was unveiled in 1982 and has a circular design meant to represent the hole down which Alice followed the rabbit in *Alice's Adventures in Wonderland*. Carroll was educated at Rugby and Christ Church, Oxford, where he became a mathematics lecturer. In addition to his humorous and imaginative stories, he also published on mathematics, including an important work, *Euclid and his Modern Rivals (1879)*.

A family memorial pays tribute to three sisters, all of whom wrote best-selling and lasting novels: **Charlotte Bronte** (1816–1855), **Emily Bronte** (1818–1848) and **Anne Bronte** (1820–1849). Their Irish father, Patrick Bronte, was perpetual curate of Haworth in Yorkshire. He had two other daughters and a son, Branwell.

Charlotte was five years old when their mother died. She became a teacher and later a governess and then, with her sister, Emily, went to Brussels to study languages (Emily and Anne also worked as governesses). In 1846 the three sisters wrote a book of poetry which they published under male pseudonyms. Charlotte's novel, *Jane Eyre*, and her sister Emily's novel, *Wuthering Heights* were both published in 1847 and the following year Anne's novel, *The Tenant of Wildfell Hall*, was published. But tragedy was soon to strike as their brother, Branwell, died of consumption in September of that year. Emily died shortly afterwards and Anne the following year. Charlotte, alone of six children, survived, her two elder sisters having died many years before. She married her father's curate in 1854 but her happiness was not to last, as she died a few months later. The three sisters were commemorated in Poets' Corner when a discreet tablet was erected in 1939 but not unveiled until after the war, in 1947.

The Bronte sisters share a small tablet close to Shakespeare.

George Eliot (1819–1880) – the male pseudonym for Mary Ann Evans – was the next female writer to have a Poets' Corner memorial; it was unveiled in 1980 on the centenary of her death. She lived with the writer, George Henry Lewis, from 1854 until he died in 1878, but never married him. Author of *Adam Bede* (1855), *The Mill on the Floss* (1860) and *Silas Marner* (1861), her *Middlemarch* (1871–2) and *Daniel Deronda* (1874–6) were published in instalments. She married in 1880 and died later the same year. The quotation on her stone is taken from her *Scenes from Clerical Life* (1858): 'The first condition of human goodness is something to love; the second something to reverence.' She is buried in Highgate Cemetery.

The lantern-jawed bust of the devoted horseman, Adam Lindsay Gordon.

Other writers from this period buried or memorialised here include:

Robert Browning (1812–1889) and his wife **Elizabeth Barrett Browning** (1806–1861). They eloped in 1846 and lived in Italy until her death in 1861 when he returned to London. His works include his volume of poems, *Asolando*, published the day he died. He is buried in the Abbey and the name of his wife, who is buried in Italy, was added to his gravestone in 1906.

A wall-mounted bronze medallion portrait head of the great social reformer, **John Ruskin** (1819–1900), is by the entrance to St Faith's Chapel on the south wall. Educated at Christ Church, Oxford, he lectured on architecture and painting. The first volume of his famous *Modern Painters* was published in 1847 – the rest were published over the next 17 years – and in 1849 he published his *Seven Lamps of Architecture*. He inherited a large fortune from his father which he gave away, mostly to philanthropic causes. Though he was offered burial in the Abbey, he said he wanted to be buried where he lived, in Coniston in the Lake District.

Matthew Arnold (1822–1888), poet, essayist and critic, was the son of the Headmaster of Rugby School, Thomas Arnold, and was educated at Rugby, Winchester and Balliol College, Oxford. He became a Fellow of Oriel College and was Professor of Poetry at Oxford from 1857–1867 and wrote on politics, religion and education. His bust, by Alfred Bruce Joy and given by his family, was originally in the south-west tower Chapel and now sits on the window sill in Poets' Corner. Below it is a wall plaque designed by Donald Buttress which was unveiled in 1989. It bears the quote, 'Let but thy light appear and thy transfigured walls be touch'd with flame,' which are Arnold's own words in his memorial poem to the Abbey's Dean Stanley. Arnold's memorial is one of a pair with that of John Clare, also designed by Donald Buttress.

A bust of the horseman and adventurer, **Adam Lindsay Gordon** (1833–1870), was unveiled on the centenary of his birth. He was born in the Azores, educated in England and then went to Australia in 1853 as an adventurer. He believed that animals could be trained by kindness and reward rather than the whip. Much of his poetry is about horses, for example *The Sick Stockrider* and *The Ride from the Wreck*. At one point he was elected to Parliament but his true love was horses. His poetry was said to be the voice of Australia. He suffered from depression and eventually shot himself. His bust is by Kathleen Scott, widow of Scott of the Antarctic.

A floor stone by Chaucer's monument celebrates **Henry James** (1843–1916), a New Yorker by birth. He travelled in Europe and eventually settled in London and later Rye in Sussex, becoming a naturalised British subject in 1915 just before his death. His *Spoils of Poynton* reflects the life of the British upper classes. His other well known works include *The Bostonians* (1886) and *The Aspern Papers* (1888). He was awarded the Order of Merit shortly before his death.

Gerard Manley Hopkins (1844–1889) was educated at Highgate School, London, and Balliol, College, Oxford. He converted to Roman Catholicism, became a Jesuit and was ordained in 1877. He entered parish work in Liverpool and was later appointed to the chair of Greek at Dublin University. His poetry shows an innovative approach to rhythm but none of his poems was published in his lifetime. His best known work is probably *The Wreck of the Deutschland.* His memorial stone was unveiled by the Duke of Norfolk in 1975.

Among the floor stones – memorials to Henry James, Lewis Carroll and Gerard Manley Hopkins.

The historian, **F W Maitland** (1850–1906), received his floor stone in 2001. Educated at Eton and Trinity College, Cambridge, he was a barrister and distinguished legal historian – 'a scholar's scholar' – who became Downing Professor of English Law at Cambridge. Among his works is an important history of the English law before the time of Edward I. He would write standing at a desk and imagine his audience in front of him. The quotation on his stone is from his *Domesday Book and Beyond*: 'By slow degrees the thoughts of our forefathers, their common thoughts about common things will have become thinkable once more.' The Dean of Westminster at the time, Dr Wesley Carr, said he judged that 'at the beginning of the new millennium, when the question of history is intensely debated, to affirm its continuing importance was a necessary statement for the Abbey to make'. Maitland is buried in the Canary Islands.

Binyon Brooke Owen Graves ...

The War Poets

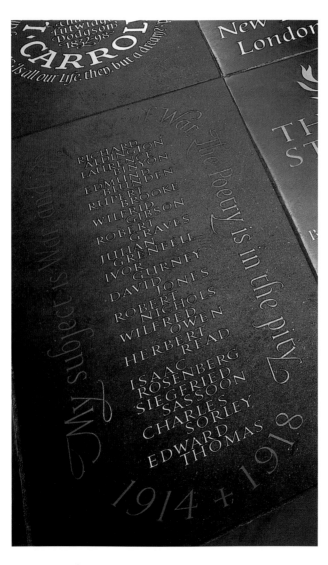

On 11 November 1985 – Remembrance Day – the Poet Laureate, Ted Hughes, unveiled a memorial in Poets' Corner to the poets of the First World War. The grey stone tablet lists 16 poets in alphabetical order. Inscribed around the edge are the words of one of them, Wilfred Owen: 'My subject is War and the pity of War. The Poetry is in the pity.'

The idea for the memorial came from the then Dean, Dr Edward Carpenter. It is one of the most evocative memorials in the Abbey and complements the grave of the Unknown Warrior at the far west end of the Abbey. The poets' works span the emotions stimulated by the 1914–18 War from the heroic glorification of conflict in the early days of battle, through gradual disillusion-ment to bitterness and desolation. Rupert Brooke (Rugby and King's College, Cambridge) and Julian Grenfell (Eton and Balliol College, Oxford) romanticised the patriotic cause. Both died in 1915. Herbert Read and

Siegfried Sassoon were among those who survived to witness and testify to the War's horror and futility. The dedication ceremony reflected the range of views when 16 of the poems were read. In his address Professor Michael Howard, Regius Professor of History at Oxford, said that the outpouring of poetry then was something which could never recur, born out of exceptional circumstances. The poets were the first people who had spoken the truth about the War – and that was the function of the poet. Dean Carpenter said of the service, 'It was an unforgettable occasion. Some in the congregation were literally weeping at the end of it.'

Perhaps the best known lines which have come down to us from that appalling time are those by **Laurence Binyon** (1869–1945) which are repeated on Remembrance Day each year as the two minutes' silence ends:

They shall grow not old, as we that are left grow old:
Age shall not weary them, nor the years condemn.
At the going down of the sun and in the morning
We will remember them.

Binyon survived the war and worked at the British Museum, eventually as keeper of Oriental prints and drawings.

Rupert Brooke (1887–1915) took part in the unsuccessful defence of Antwerp in the early days of the War and then served in the Mediterranean, where he died of septicaemia. He was buried on the Greek Island of Skyros. His famous War Sonnets include the poem, *The Soldier*, with his famous lines,

If I should die think only this of me:
That there's some corner of a foreign field
That is for ever England.

Wilfred Owen (1893–1918) enlisted in the army in 1915. Convalescing in hospital he met Siegfried Sassoon, who encouraged him in his writing. He returned to battle, won the Military Cross and was killed just one week before the Armistice – his mother received the telegram telling her of his death on Armistice Day. His best known poem is perhaps his *Anthem for Doomed Youth*:

What passing bells for these who die as cattle?
  Only the monstrous anger of the guns.
  Only the stuttering rifles' rapid rattle
Can patter out their hasty orisons.
No mockeries now for them; no prayers nor bells,
  Nor any voice of mourning save the choirs, –
The shrill, demented choirs of wailing shells;
  And bugles calling for them from sad shires.

OPPOSITE:
The names of
16 War Poets
are inscribed
on the
floor stone.

37

What candles may be held to speed them all?
Not in the hands of boys, but in their eyes
Shall shine the holy glimmer of goodbyes.
The pallor of girls' brows shall be their pall;
Their flowers the tenderness of patient minds,
And each slow dusk a drawing down of blinds.

Robert Graves (1895–1985) was badly wounded on the Somme but survived the War and was the only one of the poets still living at the time of the memorial unveiling. His First World War poems were published in 1916 but he tried to suppress them, claiming that War poems were a fashion. Another famous work of his was the novel, *I Claudius*.

Other writers contemporary with the War Poets include **Rudyard Kipling** (1865–1936), who was born in Bombay. He was the first British author to win the Nobel Prize for Literature, but he spurned the Poet Laureateship and the Order of Merit, saying he wanted no public recognition for his work. Best known among his works are his *Barrack Room Ballads* (1892), *The Jungle Book* (1894), *Kim* (1901) and *The Just So Stories* (1902). His poem, *If*, is a universal favourite.

If you can keep your head when all about you
  Are losing theirs and blaming it on you,
If you can trust yourself when all men doubt you,
  But make allowance for their doubting too;
If you can wait and not be tired of waiting,
  Or being lied about, don't deal in lies, …

which ends:

Yours is the Earth and everything that's in it,
And – which is more – you'll be a Man, my son!

Kipling retired to Sussex and wrote memorably about that county. He was buried next to Dickens and Hardy. His death coincided with that of King George V and his burial occurred on the same day that the King's body began its lying-in-state in Westminster Hall and so was eclipsed by that event. He was a dedicated Imperialist and the decline of the British Empire also served to weaken the impact of his poetry.

Thomas Hardy (1840–1928) was born near Dorchester. He began life as an architect and later wrote poems, novels and the great epic drama, *The Dynasts*. His best known titles include: *Far from the Madding Crowd* (1874), *The Mayor of Casterbridge* (1886) and *Tess of the D'Urbervilles* (18891). He was awarded the Order of Merit. His ashes are buried in the Abbey, while his heart is buried at Stinsford in Dorset.

The other War Poets on the memorial stone

Richard Aldington (1892–1962), the first-named on the stone, published several volumes of poems but was best known for his novels, including *Death of a Hero* (1929), based on his experience of the War.

Edmund Blunden (1896–1974) fought at Ypres and wrote *Undertones of War* about his experiences. He became Professor of Poetry at Oxford. One of his achievements was to research and publish previously unknown poems by John Clare.

Wilfrid Gibson (1878–1962) was a Northumberland poet and a friend of Rupert Brooke.

Julian Grenfell (1888–1915) was commissioned in the army 1910 and was killed at Ypres. His famous poem is *Into Battle*.

Ivor Gurney (1890–1937) went to war in 1915 and was wounded and gassed. He spent much of his later life in mental hospitals and died of tuberculosis.

David Jones (1895–1974) was principally a painter. He suffered from ill health and had severe nervous breakdowns. He was made a Companion of Honour for his painting talents four months before he died in 1974. His writings include *In Parenthesis* (1937), based on his experiences in the 1914-18 War, and the religious poem, *Anathemata* (1952) .

Robert Nichols (1893–1944) was educated at Winchester and Oxford. He was a Romantic in the mould of Rupert Brooke and regarded himself more as a dramatist than a poet.

Herbert Read (1893–1968) was a scholar, biographer and critic. His War poems are vivid and stark, portraying the reality of war. After the War he worked in the Victoria and Albert Museum and later became Professor of Fine Art in Edinburgh. He was knighted in 1953.

Isaac Rosenberg (1890–1918) enlisted in 1915 against his pacifist family's wishes and was killed in action. He was also a painter.

The War poems of **Siegfried Sassoon** (1886–1967) were published in 1918 in a collection called *Counter Attack*. They expressed his bitterness towards the romanticising of war.

Charles Sorley (1895–1915) was just 20 when he died, the youngest poet to be memorialised in Poets' Corner. He died in the battle of Loos, leading his company in a successful attack on a trench.

Edward Thomas (1878–1917) wrote all his war poetry from home. An artillery officer, he was killed at Arras by a shell blast.

Wilde Masefield Lawrence Thomas Eliot Auden …

Recent memorials

THOUGH TIME IS A HEALER, memorialising controversial poets long after their deaths can still lead to protests. Some were surprised when **Oscar Wilde** (1854–1900) was honoured by being included in the memorial window in 1995. His notorious homosexual lifestyle, which led him to court and eventually to a spell in jail, still raised hackles nearly a century after his death.

Educated at Trinity College, Dublin and Magdalen College, Oxford, Wilde's first book of poems was published in 1881. His best known works include *The Picture of Dorian Gray* (1891), *Lady Windermere's Fan* (1892), *A Woman of No Importance* (1893) and *The Importance of Being Earnest* (1895). His experience in jail led to two works, *The Ballad of Reading Gaol* (1898) and *De Profundis*, which was published posthumously in 1905. His imprisonment destroyed his health and he retired to Paris where he died aged 46. His name in the window was unveiled by his grandson.

While the actor Laurence Olivier was the last person to have his ashes interred in Poets' Corner, the last poet to be so honoured was **John Masefield** (1878–1967). Masefield spent part of his early life travelling in America , returning home with £6 and a revolver and vowing that he would either find work or shoot himself. Clearly he found work. He was appointed Poet Laureate in 1930. His early poems included his *Salt Water Ballads* (1902), which contain his poem, *Sea Fever*, beginning, 'I must go down to the sea again'. One of his most famous poems is *Cargoes*, the last verse of which reads:

> Dirty British coaster with a salt-caked smoke stack,
> Butting through the Channel in the mad March days,
>   With a cargo of Tyne coal,
>   Road-rail, pig lead,
> Firewood, ironware and cheap tin trays.

Meanwhile, other writers who died in the 20th century and who were buried elsewhere have received inscribed floor stones, often decades after their deaths. The memorial stone to **D H Lawrence** (1885–1930) was unveiled in 1985. The son of a Nottinghamshire miner, his parents were unhappily married and his first novel, *Sons and Lovers*, reflects that. He eloped with an older woman but their marriage fared no better. He wrote about the dark forces of nature, especially sex, and his last book, *Lady Chatterley's Lover*, was the subject of a court case during which the prosecuting counsel, Mervyn Griffith-Jones famously questioned whether it was the sort of book anyone would let his wife or servants read. Lawrence died of tuberculosis and was originally buried in France, but his body was later transferred to Taos, New Mexico, where he once lived. The decision to memorialise him in the Abbey caused a stir, one newspaper complaining that Lawrence was 'a militant proselytising pagan, bitterly opposed to everything which Christianity had to teach'. His stone depicts a phoenix rising from the ashes and the words 'Homo sum – the adventurer.'

The memorial stone for **Dylan Thomas** (1914–1953) was dedicated in 1982, nearly 30 years after his death. His 'play for voices', *Under Milk Wood*, is his best known work. Born in Swansea, he worked as a journalist and script writer in London, married and returned for a while to Wales. Thomas became a legend in his own lifetime and his poetry, full of vitality and sometimes obscure imagery, was very popular. He died in New York of alcohol poisoning. His poem addressed to his father is one of his most famous. Its first verse reads:

Flowers are often laid on poets' memorials on significant anniversaries.

Do not go gentle into that good night,
Old age should burn and rave at close of day;
Rage, rage against the dying of the light.

While these poets had to wait many years for their memorials, others were more quickly recognised. T S Eliot's stone was unveiled in 1967, only two years after his death, and W H Auden's stone, only a year after his.

Thomas Stearns Eliot (1888–1965) was the second American-born poet to be commemorated in Poets' Corner (the first being Longfellow). His memorial was unveiled by his widow, Valerie. Eliot was educated at Harvard, the Sorbonne and Merton College, Oxford. He emigrated to England in 1915 and joined Lloyd's Bank as a clerk; his first book of poetry, *Prufrock and Other Observations*, was published in 1917. He founded the *Criterion*, a literary periodical, in 1922, in which *The Wasteland* was first published. He became a British subject in 1927 and joined the Anglican church. His work, *Four Quartets*, was published from 1936 and reflected on time, place and memory – it is perhaps the greatest Christian poem of the 20th century. His children's book, *Old Possum's Book of Practical Cats*, was made into a musical by Andrew Lloyd Webber. In 1948 he was awarded the Nobel Prize for Literature and received the Order of Merit. The quotation on his memorial is from *Little Gidding*, the last of the *Four Quartets*: 'The communication of the dead is tongued with fire beyond the language of the living'.

Wystan Hugh Auden (1907–1973) lived for a time in Germany under the Weimar Republic during the rise of Nazism. He was homosexual but married a Jewish woman to save her from the Nazis. After his return to England he worked as a schoolmaster and made documentary films, but emigrated to the USA in January 1939. When war was declared in September of that year he decided to remain in America, attracting a lot of criticism back home. He took American citizenship but later he returned to England to become Professor of Poetry at Oxford University (1956–61). He is buried near Vienna, where he had a home. One of his popular poems is *Night Mail*, written for a documentary film on the London to Scotland mail train, which begins:

This is the Night Mail crossing the Border,
Bringing the cheque and the postal order,
Letters for the rich, letters for the poor,
The shop on the corner, the girl next door.

The quotation on his memorial comes from *In Memory of W B Yeats*: 'In the prison of his days teach the free man how to praise.'

In contrast to the recent tradition of floor stones, **Sir John Betjeman** (1906–1984) was honoured by recycling an 18th-century cartouche which had been found in the triforium. It was additionally adorned with a stone *Bible*,

Book of Common Prayer and bell (his autobiography was called *Summoned by Bells*), representing what was significant in his life. He was a friend to Westminster Abbey all his life and in his later years served on its Architectural Advisory Committee.

Betjeman was educated at Highgate Junior School, where he was taught by T S Eliot, and later went to Magdalen College, Oxford, where, after three years, he failed divinity and left with no degree. He developed a passionate interest in Victorian architecture and later made a name for himself as a broadcaster with his television programmes about architecture and the suburbs. His famous poem from war-time which begins, 'Come friendly bombs and fall on Slough', still gives offence to those who live there. He was made Poet Laureate in 1972. His poem, *In Westminster Abbey*, is the prayer of an upper-crust woman during wartime, the last verse of which reads:

> Now I feel a little better,
>   What a treat to hear Thy word,
> Where the bones of leading statesmen,
>   Have so often been interred.
> And now, dear Lord, I cannot wait
> Because I have a luncheon date.

Betjeman's poetry might once have saved his life. During the war he became Britain's press attaché in Dublin: at one stage he was to be the target for assassination but the project was called off because the IRA's head of civilian intelligence liked his poetry.

Unusually, Betjeman's memorial is a recycled ornate cartouche.

Gilbert Murray (1866–1957) was a distinguished scholar who did much to foster international relations. He became Regius Professor of Greek at Oxford University and was famous for his translations of Euripides' plays into English. He received the Order of Merit. His inscription translates as 'An example of true humanity, while he lived the letters of the ancient Greeks lived again, nor was there any reason to despair of the harmony of peoples.' His ashes were interred near William Camden's monument.

Alfred Edward Housman (1859–1936) was Professor of Latin at Cambridge and wrote two volumes of lyric poetry which were remarkable for their economy

43

of words: *A Shropshire Lad* (1896) and *Last Poems* (1922). His name is in the memorial window.

Ted Hughes (1930–98) was a Yorkshireman, the youngest of three children. In addition to his poems he wrote children's books, wrote and translated plays, and was a keen environmentalist. His first wife, the American poet and novelist Sylvia Plath, committed suicide in 1963. His memorial is close to that of T S Eliot, whom he described as his 'guru-in-chief'. A memorial window to the Victorian writer **Elizabeth Gaskell** (1810–65) was unveiled in 2010. Her novels reflected the different strata of Victorian society.

The most famous non-writer in Poets' Corner is the composer **George Frederic Handel** (1685–1759). His monument, by L F Roubiliac, is on the west wall and was unveiled in 1762. It is said to be modelled on his death mask – all except the ears which, in the original statue, were said to be too large and so were cut down in size. A tablet above it recalls the first Handel Festival held in the Abbey in 1784, nearly 100 years after his birth. The concerts, which included two performances of *Messiah*, were given by the largest number of musicians up to that time ever to gather under one roof: there was concern over whether the Abbey could withstand the noise and vibration.

Towards the centre of the transept is a small gravestone marking the burial place of **Thomas Parr**, a man alleged to be 152 years old when he died in 1635. He was brought to London from Shropshire by the Earl of Arundel, but lasted just two months before he succumbed to the city's germs, and died.

The memorial in Poets' Corner to the campaigner against slavery, **Granville Sharp** (1735–1813) has an effusive inscription detailing his dedicated opposition to the slave trade. It was erected by the African Institution in gratitude for his efforts. He is buried at All Saints Church, Fulham.

A door in the south wall of Poets' Corner leads to St Faith's Chapel, a place of extraordinary atmosphere where early morning prayer is said every day and where anyone may pray in peace – even when the Abbey is full of visitors.

Writers honoured elsewhere in the Abbey

Among the writers honoured elsewhere in the Abbey is **John Bunyan** (1628–1688), author of *Pilgrim's Progress*, (1684) whose commemorative window in the north transept was unveiled in 1912. He is buried in Bunhill Fields, London. Buried at the west end of the nave is **William Congreve** (1670–1729), whose plays include *The Way of the World* (1700). A bust of **Charles Kingsley** (1819–1875), a Canon of Westminster, is in St George's Chapel. His works include *The Water Babies* and *Westward Ho!*. **Isaac Watts** (1674–1748), best known for his hymns, has a memorial in the south choir aisle. **Benjamin Disraeli** (1804–1881) was a prolific writer and novelist and twice Prime Minister – once, briefly, in 1868 and then from 1874–80. He has a memorial statue in the north nave aisle. **Sir Noel Coward** (1899–1973) has a memorial floor stone in the south choir aisle on which are the words, 'A talent to amuse'.

Beneath the
memorial to
Oliver
Goldsmith,
a door leads
into St Faith's
Chapel,
reserved for
private prayer.

45

Poets and writers in Poets' Corner

Name	Dates	Buried	Memorial installed
Addison, Joseph 20	1672–1719	North aisle Henry VII Chapel	1808
Aldington, Richard 39	1892–1962	Sury-en-Vaux	1985
Anstey, Christopher	1724–1805	St Swithin's, Walcot, near Bath	1807
Arnold, Matthew 34	1822–1888	Laleham, Middlesex	Bust 1891, mural tablet 1989
Auden, Wystan H 42	1907–1973	Kirchstetten, near Vienna	1974
Austen, Jane 29	1775–1817	Winchester Cathedral	1967
Barrow, Issac 10	1630–1677	Poets' Corner	Contemporary with burial
Beaumont, Francis 10	1584–1616	Poets' Corner	Name on Cowley's gravestone
Beaumont, Sir John 10	1583–1627	Poets' Corner	No name on gravestone
Betjeman, Sir John 42	1906–1984	Trebetherick, Cornwall	1996
Binyon, Laurence 37	1869–1945	St Mary's, Aldworth, Berkshire	1985
Blake, William 26	1757–1827	Bunhill Fields, London	1957
Blunden, Edmund 39	1896–1974	Holy Trinity, Long Melford, Suffolk	1985
Bronte, Anne 33	1820–1849	St Mary's, Scarborough, Yorkshire	Erected 1939, unveiled 1947
Bronte, Charlotte 33	1816–1855	Haworth parish church, Yorkshire	Erected 1939, unveiled 1947
Bronte, Emily 33	1818–1848	Haworth parish church, Yorkshire	Erected 1939, unveiled 1947
Brooke, Rupert 37	1887–1915	Skyros, Greece	1985
Browning, Elizabeth 34	1806–1861	Protestant Cemetery, Florence	Name put on husband's stone 1906
Browning, Robert 34	1812–1889	Poets' Corner	Gravestone only
Burney, Fanny 23	1752–1840	St Swithin's, Walcot, Bath	Name in memorial window 2002
Burns, Robert 22	1759–1796	St Michael's, Dumfries	1885
Butler Samuel 16	1612–1680	St Paul's Church, Covent Garden	1721
Byron, Lord 29	1788–1824	Hucknall Torkard, Nottinghamshire	1969
Caedmon 4	c658–680	Whitby, Yorkshire	1966
Camden, William 8	1551–1623	Poets' Corner	Contemporary with burial
Campbell, Thomas	1777–1844	Poets' Corner	1848
Carroll, Lewis 32	1832–1898	Guildford Old Cemetery, Surrey	1982
Cary, Henry Francis	1772–1844	Poets' Corner	Gravestone only, inscribed 1868
Casaubon, Isaac 10	1559–1614	Poets' Corner	1634
Chaucer, Geoffrey 4	1343–1400	Poets' Corner	1556
Clare, John 30	1793–1864	St Botolph's, Helpston, Northants	1989
Coleridge, Samuel 27	1772–1834	Highgate Cemetery, London	1885
Cowley, Abraham 14	1618–1667	Poets' Corner	Contemporary with burial
Cumberland, R 23	1732–1811	Poets' Corner	Gravestone only
D'Avenant, Sir W 13	1606–1668	Poets' Corner	Gravestone only
Denham, Sir John 14	1615–1669	Poets' Corner	Name on Cowley's gravestone
Dickens, Charles 31	1812–1870	Poets' Corner	Gravestone only

Name	Dates	Buried	Memorial installed
Drayton, Michael 10	1563–1631	Poets' Corner	1720, replaced 1731
Dryden, John 15	1631–1700	Poets' Corner	Original monument replaced 1731
Eliot, George 33	1819–1880	Highgate Cemetery, North London	1980
Eliot, T S 42	1888–1965	East Coker, Somerset	1967
Fox, Adam 44	1883–1977	Poets' Corner	Gravestone only
Gaskell, Elizabeth 44	1810–1865	Knutsford, Cheshire	Name in memorial window 2010
Gay, John 18	1685–1732	Poets' Corner	Moved to triforium 1936
Gibson, Wilfrid 39	1878–1962	Cremated, ashes believed scattered	1985
Gifford, William	1756–1826	Poets' Corner	Gravestone only
Goldsmith, Oliver 22	1728–1774	Temple Church, London	1776
Gordon, Adam L 34	1833–1870	Near Melboune, Australia	1934
Graves, Robert 38	1895–1985	Deyá, Majorca	1985
Gray, Thomas 21	1716–1771	Stoke Poges, Buckinghamshire	1778
Grenfell, Julian 39	1888–1915	Military Cemetery, Boulogne	1985
Grote, George	1794–1871	Poets' Corner	Contemporary with burial
Gurney, Ivor 39	1890–1937	Twigworth, Gloucestershire	1985
Hakluyt, Richard 10	1553–1616	Poets' Corner	No marker
Hardy, Thomas 38	1840–1928	Poets' Corner (heart in Dorset)	Gravestone only
Herrick, Robert 10	1591–1674	Dean Prior, Devon	Name in memorial window 1994
Hopkins, Gerard M 35	1844–1889	Glasnevin Cemetery, Dublin	1975
Housman, A E 43	1859–1936	St Laurence, Ludlow, Shropshire	Name in memorial window 1996
Hughes, Ted 44	1930–1998	Cremated, ashes on Dartmoor	2011
James, Henry 35	1843–1916	Cambridge, Massachusetts	1976
Jonson, Ben 8	1574–1637	Nave (buried upright)	1723
Johnson, Samuel 17	1709–1784	Poets' Corner	1939
Jones, David 39	1895–1974	Ladywell Cemetery, Lewisham	1985
Keats, John 28	1795–1821	Rome	1945
Keble, John 29	1792–1866	Hursley, Hampshire	1873
Kipling, Rudyard 38	1865–1936	Poets' Corner	Gravestone only
Lawrence, D H 40	1885–1930	Taos, New Mexico	1985
Lear, Edward 32	1812–1888	San Remo, Italy	1988
Longfellow, H W 30	1807–1882	Cambridge, Massachusetts	1884
Macaulay, Thomas 30	1800–1859	Poets' Corner	1865
Macpherson, James 23	1736–1796	Poets' Corner	Gravestone only
Maitland, F W 35	1850–1906	Canary Islands	2001
Marlowe, C 9	1564–1593	St Nicholas, Deptford	Name in memorial window 2002
Masefield, John 40	1878–1967	Poets' Corner	Contemporary with burial
Mason, William 21	1725–1797	All Saints, Aston, Yorkshire	1799
May, Thomas 13	1595–1650	Poets' Corner (body later removed)	First removed. Second 1880
Milton, John 11	1608–1674	St Giles, Cripplegate	1737

Name	Dates	Buried	Memorial installed
Murray, Gilbert 43	1866–1957	Poets' Corner	Gravestone only
Nichols, Robert 39	1893–1944	Lawford, Essex	1985
Owen, Wilfred 37	1893–1918	Ors Communal Cemetery, France	1985
Philips, John	1676–1708	Hereford Cathedral	1710
Pope, Alexander 16	1688–1744	Twickenham	Name in memorial window 1994
Prior, Matthew 18	1664–1721	Poets' Corner	Contemporary with burial
Read, Herbert 39	1893–1968	St Gregory's Minster, Kirkdale, Yorks	1985
Rosenberg, Isaac 39	1890–1918	Bailleul Rd Cemetery, Flanders	1985
Rowe, Nicholas 20	1674–1718	Poets' Corner	1742 – now in triforium
Ruskin, John 34	1819–1900	Coniston, Cumbria	1902
St Denis, Charles de	1613–1703	Poets' Corner	Contemporary with burial
Sassoon, Siegfried 39	1886–1967	Mells Churchyard, Somerset	1985
Scott, Sir Walter 30	1771–1832	Dryburgh Abbey, Scotland	1897
Shadwell, Thomas 16	c1642–1692	Chelsea	Early 1700s
Shakespeare, William 6	1564–1616	Stratford-upon-Avon	1741
Shelley, Percy Bysshe 28	1792–1822	Rome	1945
Sheridan, Richard 23	1751–1816	Poets' Corner	Gravestone only
Sorley, Charles 39	1895–1915	On the battlefield at Loos	1985
Southey, Robert 28	1774–1843	Crossthwaite Church, Keswick	1845
Spenser, Edmund 5	1553–1599	Poets' Corner	1620 (replaced 1778)
Stapylton, Sir Robert 14	d 1669	Poets' Corner	Name on Cowley gravestone
Tennyson, Alfred 30	1809–1892	Poets' Corner	1895
Thackeray, William M	1811–1863	Kensal Green Cemetery, London	1865
Thirlwall, Connop	1797–1875	Poets' Corner	Contemporary with burial
Thomas, Dylan 41	1914–1953	Laugharne, South Wales	1982
Thomas, Edward 39	1878–1917	Agny Military Cemetery, Agny	1985
Thomson, James 20	1700–1748	St Mary's Church, Richmond, Surrey	1762
Triplet, Thomas 14	1601–1670	Poets' Corner	Contemporary with burial
Trollope, Anthony 32	1815–1882	Kensal Green Cemetery, London	1993
Vincent, William	1739–1815	St Benedict's Chapel	Contemporary
Wilde, Oscar 40	1854–1900	Père Lachaise Cemetery, Paris	Name in memorial window 1995
Wordsworth, W 27	1770–1850	St Oswald's, Grasmere	1854, moved to Poets' Corner 1932

"In the beginning was the Word, and it is the Word that gives life. But in the end there is silence. The silence when all our halting, approximate words, even the finest and most memorable of them, come to an end. The books are shut. Poets' Corner closes for the night. And in the ensuing silence two things remain: gratitude and wonder."

The Very Reverend Michael Mayne, Dean of Westminster 1986–96 from Pray, Love, Remember *(1998)*